Welcome

NAOMI STARKEY

I am delighted to w *Quiet Spaces*. I hav first three issues edited by Becky Winter and look forward to building on what she has established.

Our theme for this issue is 'The Garden', an image that resonates in our hearts because it has been part of us from the very beginning of creation. The articles are all linked to this theme in some way, whether literal celebrations of caring for the natural world or drawing on related ideas. We consider the consequences of the Fall, the hope of redemption, the 'fullness of life' that God has always intended for us, and how we can still sense his guiding presence us today, drawing close to us as he once drew close in the 'cool of the day' to walk and talk with the man and woman in Eden.

If you feel moved to respond to what you read, as I hope you will, please feel free to share your thoughts using the *Quiet Spaces* web forum at www.quietspaces.org.uk. This has been set up as an arena for conversation and a space for a community of readers to flourish—all it needs is you!

Naomi Starkey

1

This edition copyright © BRF 2006
Authors retain copyright in their own work
Illustrations copyright © Jane Bottomley, Chris Daunt and Ian Mitchell 2006

Published by
The Bible Reading Fellowship, First Floor, Elsfield Hall, 15–17 Elsfield Way, Oxford OX2 8FG
Websites: www.brf.org.uk and www.quietspaces.org.uk
ISBN-10 1 84101 450 8
ISBN-13 978 1 84101 450 0

First published 2006
10 9 8 7 6 5 4 3 2 1 0
All rights reserved

Acknowledgments

Scripture quotations taken from the Holy Bible, New International Version, copyright © 1973, 1978, 1984 by International Bible Society, are used by permission of Hodder & Stoughton Limited. All rights reserved. 'NIV' is a registered trademark of International Bible Society. UK trademark number 1448790.

Scripture quotations taken from The New Revised Standard Version of the Bible, Anglicized Edition, copyright © 1989, 1995 by the Division of Christian Education of the National Council of the Churches of Christ in the USA, are used by permission. All rights reserved.

Scripture quotations from THE MESSAGE. Copyright © by Eugene H. Peterson 1993, 1994, 1995. Used by permission of NavPress Publishing Group.

A catalogue record for this book is available from the British Library

Printed by Gutenberg Press, Tarxien, Malta

Quiet Spaces

CONTENTS

PLUS :

Poems, quotes and meditations

From **cradle** to **grave**

The Revd David Robertson is a vicar in West Yorkshire. After 36 years of study, he continues to find the Bible surprising, fresh and challenging. He has also written 'Marriage—Restoring our Vision' (BRF, 2005).

When we read about gardens in the Bible, we tend to look through the lens of our own experience. In our culture, the ambience of the garden is our primary focus, and we expect a place of retreat, beauty and relaxation; so when we read the word 'garden' we already have a picture in our mind of what we should be looking at. Our memory stirs, and our imagination fills with colour, scent and gentle sounds—and we impose this picture on the page in front of us. If we are not careful, though, we miss the point, because in the Bible, the focus is on events. A garden is mentioned because of what happens there.

Home
Work
Relationships

Eden, the cradle of life

Genesis 2:5–25 tells us the story of Eden, how God creates the man and then the woman, and gives them the task of cultivating the garden. For them, Eden isn't a place of relaxation, away from the drudgery of life; it's where they live all day, every day. It's their home, their place of work, and the location of their relationship with each other and with God. They are in an open, naked relationship with one another and with their creator who walks with them. They are trusting and trusted and they have permission to eat from any tree in the garden, including the tree of life (see 3:22), but with one exception: they may not eat from the tree that gives knowledge of good and evil. Eden is where the human race begins; it's the cradle of life, the location from which human beings will expand into the earth and fulfil their role as stewards. The world will be populated by a race in open, naked relationship with one another and with God, and they will discover the glories of creation as they go.

The picture of Eden painted for us in Genesis 2 is of a garden that is neither paradise nor heaven, but an earthly place. We should look at it through the lens of God's intention for the world, and we should recognize that there were other 'footprints' there besides the human or divine: the serpent lived there too. In this garden, as chapter 3 describes, human beings face temptation and, through their disobedience, it becomes the place where they destroy everything that matters to them—their relationship with one another and with God, their freedom, their rapport with creation and life itself. And when God's people look back at Eden (for example, in Isaiah 51:3; Ezekiel 28:13), they never think of it as a paradise to find, and there is no longing to return there. Rather, the garden symbolizes what has been lost. It was there that human beings had life and all that gives richness and depth to life, but chose death instead. Eden can never be regained; it is guarded and no human may go back. The only choice is to look ahead. In the future God promises life, but as a new work (Isaiah 43:19); Eden is gone and the tree of life will be located elsewhere.

An ordinary person might dream of Eden, but they could never afford to make a replica

History and romance

There is something about a garden that draws us, and in this respect we are little different from the people of the Bible. In our society, our garden might be a place of refuge and beauty, or an opportunity for home-grown produce. Whether we grow chrysanthemums or carrots, our gardens feed the heart—but we have the

Whichever garden we visit, we hear the footsteps of God

Are all gardens in the Bible overlaid with nostalgia and yearning?

luxury to choose; for the people of the Bible, their choice was defined by their wealth. The king's garden is mentioned in several passages (for example, 2 Kings 25:4 and Nehemiah 3:15), and he could afford to keep a royal garden with trees for shade and pretty plants that pleased the eye. For most people, though, their garden was their vegetable plot (see Jeremiah 29:5), and these plots should not be confused with vineyards or orchards because they were more what we would call 'market gardens' than personal spaces (Ecclesiastes 2:4–5).

There were three different types of garden. The very wealthy could, like the king, afford to set aside land within the walls of their home to make a private garden. The moderately wealthy could afford to make a garden on land near their home, which they would visit in the cool of the evening. It was to this kind of garden, on the Mount of Olives, that Jesus and the disciples went after their Passover meal. For everyone else, their garden was where they grew herbs, vegetables and maybe some fruit. Certainly we find in the Bible the expectation that gardens will be places of retreat and relaxation, but we also see a social truth: in a fallen world, this kind of leisure costs money. Only the wealthy could afford the luxury of a 'non-productive' garden. For most people, the idea of sitting in a lovely garden was just that—an idea. An ordinary person might dream of Eden, but they could never afford to make a replica.

Similarly, the languid romance of the Song of Songs uses the image of a garden, with its heady scents and colours, to express the iridescent emotions of the lovers (especially in chapters 4—6). As we read these poems, we can almost hear the bees buzzing in the pheromonal flowering of erotic love! By setting the poems in a garden, the writer is also giving us an overtone of Eden, and perhaps we should see the love shared in marriage as the new cradle of life. As the man and woman walk together in this fallen world, their marriage relationship becomes the 'garden' in which human beings seek to obey the original commandment of God to be fruitful and multiply.

So, is that it? Are all gardens in the Bible overlaid with nostalgia and yearning? No, because there are two more gardens that need exploring, and both were visited briefly by Jesus.

Whether we grow chrysanthemums or carrots, our gardens feed the heart

Gethsemane and the garden of the tomb

It was in Gethsemane that Jesus wrestled in prayer as the thought of what lay ahead threatened to crush him (see Matthew 26). It was here that Jesus faced his final temptation and submitted to the will of his Father. It was here that he was betrayed and arrested. This garden was no paradise, and on the night of Jesus' arrest many different feet walked there. There was no serpent, but there was Judas, along with large crowds of people including priests, temple guards, disciples, slaves and wailing women. Jesus walked freely into a quiet garden to pray; he walked out between armed guards among a clamouring mob, and this was just a foretaste of what was to come.

After the trial, the baying of the crowds, conviction, abuse and execution, Jesus was laid to rest in a garden tomb (see John 19). It wasn't unusual for tombs to be located in gardens, and we see a reference to this in

Jesus walked freely into a quiet garden to pray

The garden symbolizes what has been lost

the burial of Amon, in 2 Kings 21:26. For Jesus, though, the tomb was borrowed and its use was prompted by the impending sabbath. It isn't clear whether Joseph intended the tomb to be Jesus' final resting place or a temporary solution until an alternative could be found. If the latter is true, then Mary's words to Peter in John 20:2 mean, 'Joseph and Nicodemus have taken the Lord, and we don't know where they have put him!' What is clear, though, is that this garden also experienced many footsteps, including those of the Roman guards and angelic visitors. As the events lead to a climax, we see creatures of earth meeting creatures of heaven as the one who centres all of creation, the man who is God, or the God who became man, rises from death and the re-creation begins.

Three gardens, one message

As we look at Eden, Gethsemane and the garden of the tomb, we go from humanity's cradle to its grave, and God is walking with us every step of the way. In Eden, the first Adam was tempted, and he fell when he acted according to his own desire. In Gethsemane, the second Adam—Jesus— was also tempted, but conquered when he bowed to God's desire. Both Adams left their respective gardens and met death, and for both it was the consequence of sin, but for the first Adam it was his own sin that led him to the gate of the garden. From then on, life would be hard until age and death returned him to the dust from which he had been created. For the second Adam, the garden gate also led to death—but it was the sin of every other human being in the whole of creation that led him there, not his own sin.

In Jesus the words of the prophets are fulfilled and the garden of Eden, the birthplace of humanity, is relocated. The new work of God is revealed, and the cross of Christ becomes the tree of life, the place of new birth, while the burial garden, a place of death, is

In the Bible, the important gardens are places where we begin

changed into a second cradle of life. Early in the morning, the women visit Jesus' tomb, expecting to find death. What they find, though, is life, for he is risen from the dead. Now there is eternal life for human beings, and the new cradle is our relationship with the risen Lord. The way back to Eden may be guarded, but in Jesus there is a gateway into the presence of the Father. The human race may be fallen, but we do not have to remain in the dirt; we may dwell again with God, and from now on it will be Jesus who walks with us.

Some people wish to locate Gethsemane and the garden tomb, in the same way that others wish to locate Eden, but if we focus on geography we miss the point. In all three gardens the perspective is 'inside out'. The Bible shows us what happened there, but then directs our attention to what happened next. The message is the same for all gardens, and it's this: 'Look what this means for the world!'

Jesus said to her, 'Mary!'

In the Bible, the important gardens are places where we begin. In Eden, human beings take their first few steps and stumble. In Gethsemane, Jesus walks away from self for the sake of all, and in the garden of the tomb he begins a new journey with the human race. Whichever garden we visit, we hear the footsteps of God, and each of those steps is personal.

On that first morning of resurrection, as Mary stands by the tomb, distraught and weeping, she is not alone. As she turns away from the empty burial place, she is greeted by Jesus. Mistaking him for the gardener, she asks him to tell her where the body of her Lord has gone. Jesus utters her name, and her life changes for ever. In this new cradle of life, this new Eden that is a relationship with Jesus, she is met openly, personally, by God. And maybe, in thinking that this second Adam was the gardener, she was not completely wrong! ■

As we look at Eden, Gethsemane and the garden of the tomb, we go from humanity's cradle to its grave, and **God is walking with us every step of the way**

Life to the full

Pamela Evans enjoys encouraging others in their discipleship through writing, speaking and spiritual direction. Her books, 'Driven Beyond the Call of God' and 'Building the Body', are published by BRF.

What do most people mean by living life to the full? Dancing till dawn? Travelling to exotic places? Eating, drinking and making merry? Bungee jumping? All of the above? The answer may well depend on age, physical fitness and disposable income.

For many, the idea of living life to the full is future-orientated: 'One day, I'll…' Young people fantasize about what life will be like when they're free to do as they please. Adults work hard to fund pensions, eventually facing the dilemma of whether to build bigger nest-eggs or retire before their get-up-and-go deserts them. Some eagerly anticipate the day when they'll be able to start really living, only to succumb to life-threatening illness.

When Jesus spoke of himself as the life-giving good shepherd, he set that picture alongside a description of 'the thief' who 'comes only to steal and kill and destroy' (John 10:10). Many today will dismiss the notion of being robbed by a spiritual enemy. They may, though—if pressed—admit to being dogged by life-sapping depression or anxiety. Others, forging ahead, apparently cheerfully, and declaring that the one who dies with the most toys wins, may nonetheless be wrestling with deep dissatisfaction. On gentle probing, they may confess to feeling disconnected from everything going on around them, or to a heart-numbing loneliness, which they seek to assuage in internet chat rooms or one-night stands.

The gospel message of abundant life—starting now—has obvious relevance to such 21st-century malaises. So it's sad that eternal life is often characterized as eventual life—for later, not yet. Yes, there are aspects of the life Jesus promises that will only be fully realized after death, but God didn't rescue us from the dominion of darkness and bring us into the kingdom of his Son simply to give us something to look forward to when we die. His plans for us may include world travel and good food (not so sure about the bungee jumping!) but they may not. What's certain is that they'll include fruitful participation in the life of his kingdom—oh, and a lifelong course in character transformation as well.

Are *you* being robbed?

Sadly, it's not just those outside the church who are missing out, and it's not a new problem. Centuries before Christ, when the prophet Isaiah proclaimed God's invitation to the hungry and thirsty, he posed this question: why were God's people feeding themselves the spiritual equivalent of junk food, and labouring over things that were never going to bring satisfaction, when they could be enjoying a feast for free? (Isaiah 55:1–2).

Jesus said, 'I have come that they may have life, and have it to the full'
JOHN 10:10

It's not our failings that make God gracious

and prayer feeling dry as dust; growing dependence on mood-altering substances.

Try running a mental video of your life over the past few days. Then picture the good Shepherd calling his sheep by name; the sheep attentive to his familiar voice, following because they know and trust him. Where are the similarities? The contrasts? (Does the pace of sheep following a shepherd seem awfully slow?) Don't rush on; take time to reflect.

Choosing life

As the children of Israel prepared to enter the promised land, Moses issued a challenge: 'I have set before you life and death, blessings and curses. Now choose life, so that you and your children may live and that you may love the Lord your God, listen to his voice, and hold fast to him. For the Lord is your life' (Deuteronomy 30:19–20).

Each of us must also 'choose life', accepting Christ as our Saviour and Lord. But in addition we must choose to follow day by day, if we're to be in the right place to receive all the nourishment, protection and other blessings the good Shepherd has for us.

About 30 years after Jesus' crucifixion, Peter found it necessary to remind his fellow Christians of how they'd been 'redeemed from the empty way of life handed down' to them by their forefathers (1 Peter 1:18). Paul chided the Colossians for having such low expectations of life in Christ. THE MESSAGE version tells it straight: 'You don't need a telescope, a microscope, or a horoscope to realize the fullness of Christ, and the emptiness of the universe without him. When you come to him, *that fullness comes together for you, too*' (Colossians 2:9, my italics).

Ironically, a full life can be one of the most effective distractions from Jesus' gift of life to the full. Jam-packed schedules leave some well-meaning Christians so drained by 'hurry sickness' that they overlook danger signals: the squeezing out of opportunities for fellowship and mutual encouragement; Bible reading

Enjoying a climate of grace

Many outside the church cannot imagine life under God's rule as anything other than a joyless slog punctuated by frequent exhortations to shape up and do better. What a travesty!

1 Peter 5:10 calls God 'the God of all grace'. Unfortunately, his grace is often explained in terms of our unworthiness: God goes on loving and giving even though we don't deserve it. This is true! But it's not our failings that make God gracious. His grace—his love-in-action, creating, redeeming, empowering, comforting and much more—is a revelation of his essence, his character. He is full of grace because the God of all grace cannot be otherwise, and the atmosphere of his kingdom reflects this grace.

For those with eyes to see, signs of what God is like are close at hand. Have you ever been touched by the deep colours in a sunset? By sunlight reflected in dewdrops on a spider's web? Have you found strength, wisdom or other resources you didn't know you had, just when you needed them? Have you met 'the God of surprises' in unexpected places—in the supermarket, a hospital ward or a train? If you have yet to experience anything similar, try praying, 'Lord, give me eyes to see…'.

You've probably heard of followers of Jesus, imprisoned for their faith, bringing a climate of grace to their prison cell. In this way, they've been able to offer guards and fellow inmates alike a glimpse of the one they serve, and a breath of 'fresh air'. Within God's kingdom, kindness, compassion and forgiveness for one another are the norm, whatever the surroundings—as normal as bitterness, anger and slander are where the Enemy is determining the climate. Who's controlling the climate where you are?

Living the life

God's plan is that, instead of allowing the world to go on imprinting us with its patterns, we cooperate with him as he renews us from the inside out. 'We have the mind of Christ,' wrote Paul, and then challenged Corinthian Christians about their quarrelling (1 Corinthians 2:16b—3:3). You're probably aware of ways in which you fail to reflect the image of Christ.

For those with eyes to see, signs of what God is like are close at hand

I certainly am. But in terms of good and bad habits, those we practise grow stronger, so let's practise the good ones! 'Train yourself to be godly,' Paul urged Timothy (1 Timothy 4:7). Our daily 'working out' of what God has 'worked in' (Philippians 2:12–13) pleases God and makes us more fruitful. As a bonus, we find ourselves more at home in the kingdom climate.

Writing about Jesus' paradoxical teaching that we must lose our lives if we are to find them (Matthew 16:25), theologian and philosopher Dallas

Lord, lead me deeper into Life today

Willard says that 'life as normally understood, where the object is securing myself, promoting myself, indulging myself, is to be set aside'. He goes on, '"Can I still *think* about such things?" you may ask. Yes, you can. But you increasingly won't' (*Renovation of the Heart*, NavPress, 2002).

Meditating on the scriptures, alone and with others who are seeking to move on with the good Shepherd; revelling in creation while worshipping the Creator; listening to God in Spirit-directed prayer—these and other spiritual disciplines will allow the mind of Christ to hold greater sway within us, and they'll expand our horizons in life-enhancing directions.

I find the Lord's Prayer helpful, not least as an aid to remembering whose will is to be done, whose kingdom rule I'm committed to welcoming, and whose is the power and the glory. Psalm 23 is another rich resource for present-day 'sheep'. Try reflecting on it, praying, 'Lord, lead me deeper into Life today.' Savour the images of faithful nurturing, wise guidance, strong protection and eternal security, and your relationship with the Shepherd will be strengthened, your trust in his goodness and love will grow, and your character will be nourished by his.

Finding fulfilment

Those who accept that Jesus offers not only a kind of life that serves God's purposes, but also one that is truly fulfilling, and who daily choose to live in the light of that acceptance, find freedom and satisfaction. For two thousand years, saints have testified that this is so. Are you able to do the same?

Thinking about the most fulfilled people I know, I can see that they've attuned their ears to the good Shepherd's voice and are happy to be following his lead. Each is glad to be identified as 'God's workmanship, created in Christ Jesus to do good works' (Ephesians 2:10). Their activities are as varied as they are. But what's striking is that such people know truly how to *be*. This influences not only what they do but also how they do it: their doing is characterized by God's *shalom* peace, not anxious striving. At home in a climate of grace, they 'grace' others as part of normal living.

Are they living 'life to the full'? I think they are. Is this what our friends and neighbours need? I think it is. Want to know how to reveal more of it to them? Ask the good Shepherd! ■

Once upon a time there was a garden…

Naomi Starkey is the editor of 'Quiet Spaces'. She also edits 'New Daylight' Bible reading notes, as well as commissioning BRF's books for adults.

> **Remember— change is a sign of life**

It was the dead of January. As the gardener looked around, her heart sank. A waist-high sea of dead nettles filled half of what could have been a lawn. On either side were beds choked with brambles and monstrously overgrown shrubs. Two unkempt apple trees leaned towards each other at an awkward angle, while in the background a rickety fence could be glimpsed through swathes of ivy. Lined up at either end, like sentinels of decay, were a shattered greenhouse and a lopsided shed.

And that was just the back garden. The front was dominated by a yew tree that shadowed half the house so that the bricks were green with mould. There was also a vast lime tree that littered the crumbling drive with dead branches. Over the door, clinging to a tangle of wires and rusty nails, was a climbing rose, one living stem amid a cluster of sticks.

'Why on earth did I decide to come?' the gardener asked herself. Unfortunately, that was a rhetorical question—she could remember why all too easily. There had been that moment, four months ago, when she heard, quiet but unmistakable, the voice of God: 'I want you to work here.' Her response had been a glib 'OK!' as she strolled back to her car through the sunshine, thinking that there was a lot of work to do, but such potential! Now it all felt very different.

At first, the transformation felt easy, if arduous. She sharpened a scythe and swept away the field of nettles. She removed heaps of old prunings and lopped the branches overhanging the fence from next door. In the greenhouse she found ancient sacks of compost that disintegrated as she tried to lift them. The shed was so crammed with rubbish that at first she could not get inside at all. When she forced a way through, she faced coils

It was as if she had reached the bones of the garden, the bare foundations

of rotting rope, bags of fossilized jumble, packing cases stuffed with 20-year-old newspapers.

All the rubbish went to the tip, as did the dismantled shed and even the greenhouse in due course. 'I'm getting somewhere!' she said to God excitedly, as she surveyed the cleared site. There seemed so much that she

could do, given time—and just a little more effort. Maybe by July it would all be finished…

When she began digging the ground, it was like chipping at concrete. The hard-packed soil was littered with stones, broken bricks, clinker from long-ago coal fires. To keep herself going, she made herself cultivate just one row, and then another, then another, inching her way along the border. Sweat trickled down her back as she hacked away with her spade.

When she worked at the front, she was further discouraged by some of the comments of passers-by.

'That rose over the door was always so lovely. I suppose you're thinking of chopping it all down?'

'Where have all the old wallflowers gone?'

'I do think gardens look better when they are a bit free and wild. So *suburban* to have it all trimmed and tied down…'

'Why can't they see that this is nothing but neglect and ugliness?' she said to God, angrily. 'They are saying that I would be better off leaving it alone.'

There was stillness, and God replied: 'Remember—change is a sign of life. But many people do not like change.'

When spring came, the garden looked worse, not better. The lime tree burst into leaf and began weeping a sticky rain over those plants not blighted by the deep, dry shade of the yew tree. Everywhere the gardener turned, she found weeds sprouting. As she tackled them, they stung her face,

scratched her arms and pierced her leather gauntlets.

Foraging in the undergrowth, she found some plants that she could nurse back to health—but many were beyond rescue. She transplanted an old rose bush from beneath a tumbledown buddleia, and at first it eagerly produced shoots. Then the new leaves began to wilt, no matter how much she watered it, and in the end it became a thorny stick that she had to dig up and discard, like so much else.

The garden that she had dreamed was beginning to emerge

At the end of the first summer, when she saw how much ground remained untouched, she felt a twinge of despair.

'I'm worried, God,' she said as she pulled on her boots for a session of muck-spreading. 'Am I wasting my time? Isn't this a job for a professional team?'

She picked up her spade and set to work in silence. Then God spoke, infinitely patient: 'Do one job at a time. More clearance must happen before the planting can begin.'

At times her efforts left the place looking more of a mess than ever. The larger of the two apple trees, for example—she went at it with a saw during the second winter and it was left with just a few branches poking into the grey sky, like something from the ape house at the zoo.

'Where are you going with this?' a friend asked, as they stared out from the kitchen window.

'It's revolution, not evolution,' said the gardener, trying to disguise her uncertainty as to whether she had done the right thing.

'I don't know why you bother,' her friend replied. 'It wasn't as if it was so bad before—it had a certain overgrown charm.'

'Like a disused graveyard, you mean,' the gardener said crossly. The next day she chopped down the other apple tree, which had proved blighted and fruitless over the past year, digging away at the stump until it came free, leaving a patch of trampled mud like a scene from a battlefield.

That winter she dug and forked and manured until sometimes she could hardly walk afterwards. It was as if she had reached the bones of the garden, the bare foundations, as she raked the soil over and over until it lay as finely crumbled as brown sugar. When at last the time came for planting, she applied water, fertiliser, compost and set out shrub after shrub, small and spindly-looking in the wide, empty beds, as well as shaking out a good many packets of seeds.

In the second summer, she was rewarded by a host of poppies and cornflowers that flourished for a few weeks. All too quickly, though, it was autumn and then winter again, and she started digging, raking and levelling once more, as well as planting sackfuls of bulbs—daffodils, snowdrops, crocuses, tulips.

In the third spring, she drank tea with another friend on the bumpy lawn, trying to enjoy the garden a little rather than simply treating it as a workplace. Her friend had brought along an overexcited toddler, and the gardener shuddered as he galloped between the young lavender bushes.

'I can see you've got a lot of work to do here,' her friend commented brightly, catching the child as he advanced upon a tulip. The gardener forced a smile.

Later she told God that she had had enough: 'I think it's time for me to move on and try somewhere else. Things will never be more than mediocre here.'

'You saw the potential before,' God answered. 'And that has not changed.'

'Well, I'm too tired to realize it.'

'Look around and see how much you have achieved already.'

The gardener shook her head. 'All I can see is how much still needs to be done.'

Change is a sign of life

But many people do not like change

God's reply was so quiet that she could barely hear it: 'I know that you are the best person to do this.'

That third autumn, she took the front garden in hand. The huge trees were pruned back to a manageable shape, and at last the sunlight could break through. As the warmer weather came, the climbing rose round the door burst into bloom. And to her astonishment the house bricks began to change colour, from green to rosy pink.

The months passed. Another spring came, another summer and autumn. The pruned shrubs grew with greater vigour. The new planting became established. The gardener began to sense a change—she was now trimming and tidying what was there rather than breaking new ground and digging up roots. Then it was January (her fifth New Year in that place), February, March—and suddenly she looked at the garden and saw that the end of her battle was in sight. Yes, the lawn still contained as much dandelion as grass. There were gaps where plants had died instead of flourishing in their new home, but the garden that she had dreamed was beginning to emerge.

And then it was early June. The gardener lounged in a hammock one evening, swifts swooping overhead as the sun sank behind the trees. In the stillness, she sensed the presence of God beside her, looking with her at the growing garden.

'You have done well,' she heard God say. 'It is the end of the beginning.'

She sighed a little at that, but smiled as well. 'When will it be finished?'

'One day you will know when your part in it is finished.'

'What if I get too tired to do any more? What if I run out of ideas?'

'Enough questions,' said God. 'Now is the time to rest.'

God had spoken. Obediently, the gardener lay back and relaxed for what felt like the first time in four and a half years, as the night scents of the plants rose around her and the first stars appeared in the darkening sky. ■

For my soul there is a season:
A time for renewal,
For passion,
For quick and sudden growth,
For budding and blossoming.
Then God must tame my wildness,
Lest strength be expended
With the passing of spring.

For my soul there is a season:
A time of fullness,
Of beauty,
Establishing and affirming
The promise of all good things.
But of danger too, from the enemy's attack,
To spoil and destroy
All that summer brings.

For my soul there is a season:
A time for fruitfulness,
Full bodied,
Ripening and bountiful,
Harvesting and rejoicing.
When hope becomes experience,
God's blessing is poured out
And the rich fruits of autumn
Are gathered in.

For my soul there is a season:
A time of bleak darkness,
Cold winter,
When life fills with sadness
And all hope lies dying.
But do not fear
The silence of winter
For it does not speak of death,
Only of waiting.

BARBARA PARSONS

Faith

in the nursery

Martyn Payne is a member of BRF's Barnabas Ministry Team, working in schools and churches, with teachers, children's leaders and children. Martyn has also worked as the National Children's Work Co-ordinator for the Church Mission Society and, before that, taught in schools in London for 18 years.

Most of us know that many young plants must start their life within the confines of a nursery, if they are to stand any chance of reaching maturity. It comes as no surprise, then, that similar wisdom should apply to the nurture of our human young.

In recent years there has been a welter of government legislation concerned to keep children safe from harm. It goes without saying that we want the best and safest environment for our children to grow up in. Children are, after all, vulnerable members of our society. Jesus was quick to remind his listeners of this fact, and he had dire warnings for those who sought to harm 'these little ones'. Many children's leaders or potential leaders may feel that these rules and regulations have become a millstone around their necks—but interestingly, Jesus' millstone is reserved for those who don't pay due heed to these matters.

The young plant analogy for children is not the whole story, though. We can't expect to 'nursery out' all possible dangerous influences away from our children. From real nursery hotbeds we might

Are there only certain Bible stories that are safe for the young?

produce well-trained blooms that win prizes at the local flower show, but will we grow creative, mature and, most importantly, spiritually alive adults by the same process? Without some dangers there can be no true learning; without some unsupervised

Children

have less difficulty in holding together paradoxes

play there may be limited imaginative development. It becomes a tricky balance between the safety of the nursery and the wildness of the open countryside, as any caring parent knows, and it calls for much wisdom and prayer.

Does this apply to children's spiritual growth too? Are there, for example, only certain Bible stories that are safe for the young, while others are far too dangerous to handle—maybe even for adults? Here we encounter a real issue. The Jesus who warns us to be alert to the vulnerability of children also reminds us that those very

same children have insights into spiritual truths that are hidden from the wise of this world. In other words, children can often be more clear-sighted about matters of faith than those who care for them! This is why Jesus urges us to become like them. This turns the whole nursery idea on its head. The seedling can be wiser than the mature flower! Many of us who work with children will agree with the writer of Psalm 8 that 'out of the mouth of babes and infants' God does indeed 'bring forth mature praise'.

Where does this leave us when it comes to passing on our Christian story to children? What about the more challenging doctrines of our faith? What about the more disturbing parts of the story of Jesus himself—the blood and the brutality of Easter, or some of the violent Old Testament stories? It is sometimes these very stories that get airbrushed out of what we present to children or, at the very least, sanitized so that the true force of the original story is lost. Is this good nurture of our young, or are we in danger of misrepresenting our Christian story, which may have repercussions later? After all, scripture is God's story played

out in the real world, and it is in that real world that our children grow up.

All this may explain why the range of Bible stories we use with children tends to be limited and therefore disjointed. It is interesting to note, however, that the most popular Old Testament story used with children is Noah's ark, which is, at heart, a disturbing story of judgment and yet one considered 'safe' because of the animal factor—arguably not its main point. The truth is that children can both understand and deal with a lot more than adults often realize, and what they don't need to understand at any given time they simply won't ask about yet. When they do ask, that is the time to join them on a journey of

Without some risks there is no real growth

discovery, going as far as they want to go. This will often be into uncharted waters for us too and indeed we may well need 'a little child to lead us' (Isaiah 11:6). In this respect, children are more capable of handling some important

See also the Barnabas website for various articles on working with children written by members of the team (**www.barnabasinchurches.org.uk**)

Adult markers as to when a child is 'converted' can be very unhelpful

spiritual tools than we are as adults, namely the fact that they have less difficulty in holding together paradoxes, accepting mystery and using their imaginations to contain glorious impossibles!

A child will grow in faith by stages, and as adults we are often too quick to impose either nursery limits or specific growing targets for them. Children's growth in faith is quite different. For example, adult markers as to when a child is 'converted' can be very unhelpful. Our duty is to present the whole story—the facts about Jesus and the kingdom—using appropriate language and images as with any audience, and as we share the story, God's Spirit will draw children ever deeper into his love. They will discover that God is a strong friend who keeps them safe; that God is love—an unchanging and forgiving love. In time they will discover that God hears and answers prayer; but also that

God doesn't answer all prayer, out of love for us; that God's love went to the cross to break the power of evil; that we are all part of that evil but can also become part of the glory; that God gives us his Holy Spirit to make us into the sort of person God created us to become. As we share this with children, they will respond to it at whatever stage they can. And, more remarkably, we will also receive from them help for our faith. Jesus says that as we receive children, we also receive him and God who sent him.

The key to all this is exactly what we mean by 'nursery'. Rather than a controlled environment that excludes all dangers, let us think of the nursery as 'a safe place where children can ask questions'. What defines the boundaries of this nursery is the revelation of God's truth to us through the Bible—yes, the whole story—and, within this circle of inspired truth, children can explore what they need to hear and receive, as and when they are ready. In this nursery of faith, we share with the children as equal partners, as mysteriously the seeds of faith in young and old alike mature and blossom to fill God's re-creation garden with new life. ■

I sat staring at the computer screen with tears streaming down my face. I was about to do the most difficult thing I had ever done. I had decided to offer my resignation from the post I had held in my local church for upwards of 20 years. It was a very sad situation, in which I was not without fault, but I could not accept the way in which it was being handled. I wanted to resign so that the constraints of employment law need no longer apply and we could meet together in repentance, seeking mutual forgiveness within the love of God.

I was passionate about my work and I had no idea what I would do instead. Financially I needed to earn and because I had poured so much into my church life I believed I was unemployable elsewhere.

Before starting to type, I decided to check my e-mails. I had written to my brother some ten days before, telling him of the possibility of my resignation. As I went online, a message that he had 'sent' a few days previously appeared on my screen. In it he told me of his decision to resign from a position he had held in his own church. He felt strongly that there was no way to go on with things as they were, for reasons

Under the guiding hand of God

Anne Roberts is a freelance writer and also works in Further Education and church administration. She is a contributor to BRF's 'New Daylight' Bible reading notes and lives in Bolton.

similar to mine, and that I was right to resign too.

This 'coincidence', which had caused my tears, was too much, in my estimation, to be anything but God's 'yes' to my decision. I wrote my letter of resignation. Opinion was divided as to whether or not I had been right to resign, but through the trauma of the ensuing months, I never doubted it.

I received over 100 messages from folk within the church—flowers, cards, money. On numerous occasions when I was particularly distressed, the phone or doorbell would ring, or a card drop through the letterbox. Some of the phone calls were from friends in other places who did not usually ring us. Some had no idea what had happened, until I burst into tears and explained what was going on.

I had never given much thought to angels before, but now they seemed to be popping up everywhere! I read *Miss Garnet's Angel* by Sally Vickers and, while it is only a novel, I felt a resonance with much of what it says, and sympathy with the idea of angels being around and bringing something of God's presence to us. We had a brief holiday in west Cumbria and I noticed, for the first time, the angel windows in Muncaster Church—St Michael and All Angels. I began to recognize friends as angels, or as sent by angels. My theology falls apart here, as it does for many Protestants—we're not quite sure what to make of the idea—but it held conviction for me during those months. I rethought the 'Footprints' poem. For me in my time of anguish the sand was littered with the footprints of angels—'ministering spirits sent to serve those who will inherit salvation', as Hebrews 1:14 says. There may be a misperception that God sends his angels to people of great faith, and that to claim their ministry is to claim to

There is a peace we can enjoy, even in not knowing

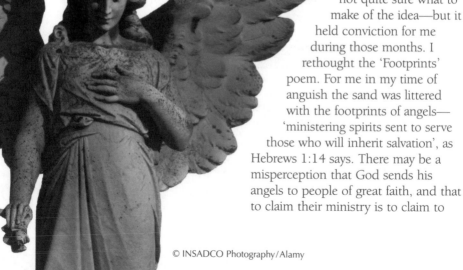

have great faith. On the contrary, I believe that God sends his angels at times when we are closest to giving up on faith. We come to the end of ourselves and our resources, even those spiritual resources that we have rightly stored up in our years of Christian discipleship. When we are left with nothing that comes near to meeting our distress, God has his opportunity. I remember, one day, feeling that no pit could be deeper than the one I was in, but clearly sensing that God was still underneath me. I was certainly not an example of quiet patience and calm under affliction. I 'lost my cool' and had to apologize on several occasions, and this only added to my distress. Again, God knew my heart and did not withdraw his loving presence.

I took on some domestic work for three elderly women. I began to write and was amazed to have work accepted immediately. I joined the exam invigilation team at a local college. To my further amazement I secured a tutoring post and, later, lecturing posts in various subjects in Further Education.

I began to recognize that my church work had meant far too much to me and that my relationships within it were no longer doing me any good: in fact, they were crippling me. I began to sense a new freedom that I had not known for some years. I enjoy my college work, most of the time, and it has led me into relationships with needy teenagers and super colleagues. Even the 18-mile drive over the west Pennine moors is a delight—in most weather conditions.

I feel able to use the expression 'a severe mercy' to describe what has happened and have been greatly helped by the words of Kurt Vunnegut, quoted by Michael Mayne in *Learning to Dance*, 'Unanticipated

> **I believe that God sends his angels** at times when we are closest to giving up on faith

invitations to travel are dancing lessons from God' (DLT, 2001). It's a slow process. I am very clumsy, spiritually speaking, but these are not private lessons and God choreographs people and angels to perform a dance that is pleasing to him.

There is a natural tendency, when something goes wrong, to question all that went before. A relationship ends in acrimony; a job becomes a nightmare; we are sure of God's will but others do not see things the same way. Living under the guiding hand of God does not make us infallible. If we think it does, we put ourselves in danger, at a later date, of questioning his love and even the word of scripture when things go pear-shaped. We must hold all things lightly. If God has to prise them away from us, there will be a deep and painful wound, which may take a long time to heal,

In my time of anguish the sand was littered with the footprints of angels

Again I am grateful to Michael Mayne for a quotation, this time from the poet Rainer Maria Rilke.

I would like to beg you… to have patience with everything that is unsolved in your heart and to try to cherish the questions themselves… Do not now search for the answers which cannot be given you because you would not be able to live them. It is a matter of living everything. Live the questions now. Perhaps you will then gradually, without noticing it, on a distant day live right into the answer.

THIS SUNRISE OF WONDER (FOUNT, 1995), P. 3

Valuable lessons do not come easily

but heal it will, although perhaps completely only in eternity. We may never know all the answers to our 'why?' but there is a peace we can enjoy, even in not knowing.

God has a unique plan for each of us. He sees the end from the beginning; we do not. The particulars of your life, and those often-painful experiences through which he will fulfil his purpose in making you more like his Son, are very different from mine. Any experiences, any doubts, any failures that show us more of ourselves and our own need of God will ultimately lead us closer to him if we will live with them.

The place at the centre of God's will is a spiritual battlefield. It is when there is most to fight for and most to learn that we find life's most valuable lessons, and valuable lessons do not come easily. The apostle Paul never hesitated to share the trials and tribulations of living in the centre of God's will. He told believers that not until we are clothed with our heavenly dwelling shall we cease to groan under the burden of our earthly tent. In the meantime, 'we live by faith, not by sight' (2 Corinthians 5:1–7). ∎

See the angel windows in Muncaster Church online at www.visitcumbria.com/wc/chc4.htm

The Colour of Repentance

Lord, in watching and waiting
I lay myself open to your call.
In receiving you I receive all.

Yet I am like a small
vase that remains empty
under the strong force
of the water that gushes
from a tap without remorse.

Be gentle with me.
If you come in mercy,
drop by drop, like the rain,
I shall receive what I can contain.
Even a small vase can hold violets
and keep them freshly in bloom,
so that the colour of repentance
may grace a room.

Violets are not flamboyant;
They grow close to the ground,
quietly concealed
by leaves at the foot of the birch.
They are not easily found.
Only to one who will search
carefully, who kneels to gaze,
is the heart of the flower revealed
against a purple frame,
its white rays
shaped like the wings of a bird,
its golden spur like a flame.

JUDITH PINHEY, FROM 'THE SONG OF HOPE' (BRF, 2002)

Music for the soul:

'In a Monastery Garden'

Gordon Giles is vicar of St Mary Magdalene's Church, Enfield, north London. He contributes to BRF's 'New Daylight' notes and has also written 'The Music of Praise' (2002), 'The Harmony of Heaven' (2003) and 'O Come, Emmanuel' (2005) for BRF.

Monasteries can seem romantic, removed places, reverberant of authentic **spirituality and prayer**

If gardens can be places of relaxation, rejuvenation and restfulness, you might think that the most spiritual of gardens could be found in a monastery. Surrounded perhaps by high walls for seclusion, a cloistered garden can still be an Eden, keeping the world out and protecting the paradise within. Viewers of the TV series that followed the fortunes of five men who voluntarily submitted themselves to monastic life will remember the impact that such a secluded community can have, in some cases enabling major changes in spiritual direction.

Monasteries can seem romantic, removed places, reverberant of authentic spirituality and prayer. While Christians and non-Christians alike may feel this, the reality does not always match the ideal, as any monk or nun will testify. Nevertheless, the monastic life commands respect and appeals even to an age of non-commitment.

It was hardly different back in 1915 when the 40-year-old English composer Albert Ketèlbey published a brief piece of music that was to earn him fame and fortune as a composer of the genre known as 'British light music'. *In a Monastery Garden* is a delightful

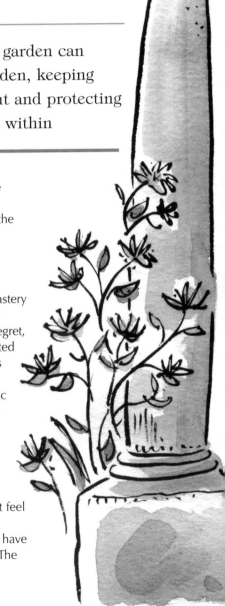

A cloistered garden can still be an Eden, keeping the world out and protecting the paradise within

evocation of the sounds of a monastic cloister. The score calls for members of the orchestra to make birdcalls, and as no choir is accommodated for in the music, the men are asked to sing the *Kyrie Eleison* ('Lord have mercy'), impersonating the chanting of monks in the distance.

Ketèlbey described the opening of his piece as representing a 'reverie in the quietude of the monastery garden amidst beautiful surroundings'. The second theme is elegiac in character, hinting at loss and regret, but in this context it has a spiritual quality associated with a sense of contrition or repentance. This gives way to the distant singing of the monks, accompanied by organ and chapel bells. The music swells as the first tune returns, and the five-minute piece concludes with what Ketèlbey called 'a glow of exultation'.

It is all very lovely, of course, and thoroughly English-sounding: melodious music, depicting beautiful surroundings, evoking a spiritual communion with nature. Today, though, we might feel that it is just too mawkish. The spirituality that Ketèlbey offers is saccharine, such that unless we have particularly sweet spiritual teeth, we may wince. The

We do need our comfort zones sometimes, our gardens of pleasure and joy

sheer loveliness of this musical meringue sounds sugary, and whips up a feel-good 'spirituality', and we may well want to ask whether this is good for us. Some people mock this kind of music, although its first hearers were moved to tears and felt that Ketèlbey really had transported them to another world, where prayer, chanting and birdsong were the only sounds to breach the holy air.

When *In a Monastery Garden* was written, World War I had begun, Impressionism was changing the world of painting for ever, and T.S. Eliot and D.H. Lawrence were writing poetry and novels. Igor Stravinsky's *The Rite of Spring* had caused a riot in Paris only a few years earlier. Ketèlbey's music was a world away from this, and he could never be described as a modernist composer, pushing the boundaries of artistic sensibility. Noticed by Elgar at the age of eleven, he soon had music published and performed widely, and he won numerous prizes and awards. His first professional post, at the age of 16, was that of organist at St John's, Wimbledon, where he established himself as a pianist and composer of church and concert music. But there was to be no career in English cathedrals for the precocious musician, as he was enticed by the world of vaudeville and light music. His reputation as a classical composer has been both burnished and, more latterly, tarnished by the rather eclectic career path that he enjoyed.

After the initial success of Ketèlbey's music, it fell out of favour and, for a few decades, was hardly heard. Recently it has gained in popularity, undoubtedly because of its irreproachable tunefulness. But the subject matter of *In a Monastery Garden*, Ketèlbey's most famous work, also reminds us that the kind of spiritual escapism that he depicts is also attracting interest. Any renewed interest in spirituality is to be cautiously applauded, and it may be that before we can be truly nourished by the Spirit of God, revealed in Christ, we need to drink the sweet milk of infant faith (see 1 Corinthians 3:1–9). Ketèlbey's portrayal of paradise confined within a cloistered garden is both appealing and appalling: like sugar, it is both good and bad for us. In such things we probably need a little moderation! Just as we cannot eat only desserts, so we cannot live for ever in a spiritual comfort zone. Yet we do need our comfort zones sometimes, our gardens of pleasure and joy, and there is nothing wrong with retreating to them from time to time; indeed, we *should* retreat to them now and again. And when we do, we can do far worse than travel to Ketèlbey's softly lilting soundworld, where, amid musical monastic reverie, we may find ourselves replenished, renewed and refreshed.

God our creator, you water the gardens of our souls with life-giving water from the spring of eternal life. Nourish us with your Holy Spirit, so that whether we need to retreat from the cares of the world or engage with them in your name, you will guide and tend us, helping us to grow in the love you have shown us in Jesus Christ our Lord. Amen

PRAYER

Readings for reflection

Genesis 2:8–17
1 Corinthians 3:1–9

Music to listen to

In a Monastery Garden by Arthur Ketèlbey (1875–1959) is the opening track on *British Light Music*, performed by the Czecho-Slovak Radio Symphony Orchestra, conducted by Adrian Leaper (Marco Polo, serial no. 8.223442). ∎

The power
of a reading Christian

Stephanie Heald is responsible for developing Spring Harvest's literary event 'A Good Read', and for the Spring Harvest publishing divison. She also speaks on workplace issues for the London Institute for Contemporary Christianity. She has helped to run a local reading group for the last three years.

Orange poppies lolling in the heat, a chilled glass of something tilting on the grass, an insect swimming frantically to cucumber for dear life. I pick up *The Time Traveller's Wife* and I'm in another garden, watching Lucille drift around in her floppy straw hat. A sunny afternoon and a good read—the perfect recipe for a sabbath rest, even for an editor!

I was once caught reading in another garden. An elderly couple padded past where I sat, and murmered, 'How very pleasant.' Excuses rushed to my defence: how industrious I really was, how rare this oasis. But it was undeniably eleven o'clock on a Monday morning, the Edinburgh Botanic Gardens could not be construed as my place of work, and I was doing nothing more productive than… reading. Like Peter Rabbit, snared by his buttons on the gooseberry net, I couldn't wriggle out of this one.

But did I need to? Must we consign reading only to holidays or hospital, bus journeys, bedtimes?

Must we devalue reading like this, as a leisure pursuit, entertainment for our free time, of which there is so little? Deceptively lovely as it is, reading is so much more than an armchair escape.

Weighed down by a summer reading list of Tolstoy and Dostoyevsky, Gogol and Pushkin, I still remember the eccentric Russian Studies lecturer's words: 'How I envy you students! You don't know how lucky you are, being paid to just read books.'

As a new editor in a religious publishing house, my lack of book-learning in the area must have shown a little. An author helpfully suggested I 'get myself a theological education'. Several mountains of good (and not-so-good) manuscripts later, I concede he was right, and hope he would now discern the beginnings of one. Books—all books—Russian literature, contemporary fiction, even or especially Christian books—have changed me. They have challenged presuppositions, opened up new worlds and ideas, grounded and strengthened my faith. Some were highlights with staggering moments of revelation, others are now a blur, but each was like a building block in a wall that the Lord continues to build.

Twenty-five years on, still paid to read books, I almost know how lucky I am.

But how to pass that knowledge on? I stand at the bookstall on Sundays, feeling like my grandfather ('You really should read more, reading broadens the mind, don't watch so much television…'), plying reluctant homegroup leaders with *John for Everyone*, worship leaders with *Distinctive Worship*, only to sell yet another copy of the one book that everyone in church has been reading for months.

Should I describe the times when life was definitely not according to plan, when crises came and rocked my faith to its core—how I clung to what I knew to be true, reminded myself of what I had learned and worked out and believed for myself, with the help of books?

Reading is one of the most neglected of spiritual disciplines

Should I describe how much easier it is to explain my faith to a friend when scriptures flood to mind, reasons, quotations and explanations thick and fast, learned with the help of books?

And how can I describe the feast there is to be had, the excitement of discovery, the new layers of truth that are uncovered as we delve deeper into our God's word, with the help of books?

Reading is one of the most neglected of spiritual disciplines. There is no material difference between listening to good preaching and reading a good Christian book. We need to invest in both, and the fruit will show. The preaching and writing of John Stott, for example, has been shaped

Reading is so much more than an armchair escape

the reviews and look at bibliographies. Look at publishers' websites and recommended reading in books you have enjoyed. Be ready to move out of your comfort zone, from the daily Bible notes to a short commentary, from a lighthearted look at the Christian life to a deeper exploration of one aspect of it. Most importantly, pray about it.

Read with others

Make friends with your local Christian bookseller, or find someone in your church who has a theological education to help you. Suggest that your homegroup read a book together each term. Best of all, start a book group. Mine began when I met for a drink with some friends and we ended up talking about what we were reading. Now we meet every couple of months, have dinner, talk about what we have read and plan what to read next. It's a lot of fun but it's also a discipline. It gives us a fixed deadline to work towards, and a chance to say what we think of a book. We have all read things we might not have chosen, but we've enjoyed the challenge of being made to think.

So take some time to dig your spiritual garden this summer: settle down with a good book! ■

and deeply affected by a reading group that met for nearly 30 years.

Here, then, are three steps to reading more.

Make time to read

Some of us will have to work hard to carve out time to read. In spite of what I have already said, the train journey may well be the only time you have to read. I always take a book with me wherever I go—so that if I have to wait in a queue I will be able at least to read. But squeezing it in isn't the ideal. Some church leaders set aside time to read each day. A friend teaches in a school where everyone, from dinner ladies to head teacher, are expected to stop and read for 20 minutes, three times a week. They can read any book they choose. The only rule is that it mustn't be related to work.

Plan your reading

Ask friends what is the most memorable book they have read. Read

Books, all books, **have changed me**

In the very
beginning

This extract presents the first reading from the revised edition of 'Faith Odyssey' (BRF, 2003) by Richard A. Burridge, a New Testament scholar and Dean of King's College, London.

Stardust and ashes

Have mercy on me, O God, according to your steadfast love; according to your abundant mercy blot out my transgressions. Wash me thoroughly from my iniquity, and cleanse me from my sin. For I know my transgressions, and my sin is ever before me…

Hide your face from my sins, and blot out all my iniquities. Create in me a clean heart, O God, and put a new and right spirit within me. Do not cast me away from your presence, and do not take your holy spirit from me.

PSALM 51:1–3, 9–11

It was a clear, starry night. I lay on my back in the grass on the top of a hill and looked up into the infinite universe above. We were out on an all-night hike with the Scouts, and someone had brought a transistor radio. The peace of the 'wee hours' was broken. 'Ground Control to Major Tom; Ground Control to Major Tom'—David Bowie's song, 'Space Oddity', drifted out towards those stars. Even if Major Tom had 'something wrong' with his spaceship, we knew then that soon our turn would come to travel out into space, on our own 'space odyssey'. Even as we watched the sky that night in the late 1960s, somewhere above us Apollo astronauts were on their way to the moon. Within a few decades, we thought we would all be able to do it, as 'scientific man' came of age and set off on the journey to the stars. We were amazed by the scientific discovery that our bodies actually contained molecules of heavy elements which had been formed within the gravity of stars. In America, hippies were celebrating at the Woodstock pop festival. Its theme song contained the chorus, 'We are stardust, we are golden, and we've got

We knew then that soon our turn would come to travel out into space, on our own 'space odyssey'

to get ourselves back to the garden'.

Yet within a few years, it was a different story. The 'love-children' at Woodstock found that they could not get themselves 'back to the garden'. The hippie dream ended bogged down in the mud of Woodstock. Love turned to violence as people were murdered while the Rolling Stones played at a subsequent concert in Altamont. Stardust had turned to ashes, the heavy molecules of long-dead stars. David Bowie changed his tune and sang 'Ashes to ashes', in which Major Tom is a junkie, 'strung out in heaven's high, hitting an all-time low'. The Apollo lunar modules and rover buggies still sit on the moon, undisturbed. We are stuck on this planet, going nowhere.

The biblical writers too reflected upon our place in the cosmos. 'In the beginning, when God created the heavens and the earth', he 'formed the man from the dust of the ground' (Genesis 1:1; 2:7). We really are created from dust and ashes, from these molecules which were formed in stars' gravities. The molecules were spread through space when the stars exploded, to end up as part of everything around us. So God warns Adam, 'You are dust and to dust you shall return' (Genesis 3:19). So when we die, we return our molecules to the universe, dust to dust, ashes to ashes. This is the paradox of human existence: we live because God has given us 'the breath of life', but this life is lived in frail bodies, earthen vessels of a few chemicals and water. We should never forget our origins. Even Abraham, the 'friend of God', when he was so bold as to plead with God not to destroy Sodom, knew his human weakness: 'Let me take it upon myself to speak to the Lord, I who am but dust and ashes' (Genesis 18:27).

No wonder that ash became a symbol of repentance, for both individuals and communities. When Job suffered his misfortunes, he 'took a potsherd with which to scrape himself, and sat among the ashes'. He blamed God, for 'he has cast me into the mire, and I have become like dust and ashes'. But when Job has finished his argument with God and heard the Lord's answer out of the whirlwind, he says, 'Therefore I despise myself, and repent in dust and ashes' (Job 2:8; 30:19; 42:6).

Fasting and being clothed in sackcloth and ashes was a way for whole communities to show their repentance. After the preaching of Jonah, 'When the news reached the king of Nineveh, he rose from his throne, removed his robe, covered himself with sackcloth, and sat in ashes' (Jonah 3:6). Jesus upbraided the towns which did not believe in him: 'Woe to you, Chorazin! Woe to you, Bethsaida! For if the deeds of power done in you had been done in Tyre and Sidon, they would have repented long ago in sackcloth and ashes' (Matthew 11:21). Peter recalls the story of Abraham and God's

We live because God has given us **'the breath of life'**, but this life is lived in frail bodies

judgment, 'turning the cities of Sodom and Gomorrah to ashes', and warns his readers to repent (2 Peter 2:6). And for all our scientific progress, we now have the capacity with our nuclear weapons to turn all our world's cities to dust and ash.

So here we are at the beginning of our journey. We recall that, despite all our great achievements, we are

Our Faith Odyssey is always a journey towards the events of **Holy Week and Easter**

poor from the dust, and lifts the needy from the ash heap' (Psalm. 113:7; 1 Samuel 2:8). The God who created us knows that 'we are but dust' and sent his Son to live among us and to raise us up, back to himself. For the ash used in Ash Wednesday services is traditionally made by burning the old palm crosses from last year. Our Faith Odyssey is always a journey towards the events of Holy Week and Easter, when we receive new palm crosses as we commemorate Jesus' death for our sin and receive new life through his resurrection. Then our ashes shall be transformed to stardust, not just 'back to the garden' but also beyond the stars 'in heaven's high'. ∎

stardust, the ashes of dead stars, formed from the dust of the ground and the molecules of the universe. People have ash put upon their foreheads in many churches as a reminder of human frailty and a sign of repentance for sin, especially on 'Ash Wednesday' at the beginning of Lent. Yet it is also a sign of hope, for God is also the one who 'raises the

For prayer and meditation
Remember you are dust, and to dust you shall return.
Turn away from sin and be faithful to Christ.
WORDS USED IN THE ASH WEDNESDAY LITURGY WHEN ASH IS PUT ON TO PEOPLE'S FOREHEADS

God Almighty planted a garden;
and, indeed, it is the purest of human pleasures.

FRANCIS BACON (1561–1626)

Of man's first disobedience, and the fruit
Of that forbidden tree, whose mortal taste
Brought death into the world, and all our woe,
With loss of Eden.

JOHN MILTON (1608–74), PARADISE LOST

Did not God
Sometimes withhold in mercy what we ask,
We should be ruined at our own request.

HANNAH MORE (1745–1833), MOSES IN THE BULRUSHES

A pity beyond all telling
Is hid in the heart of Love.

W.B. YEATS (1865–1939), THE PITY OF LOVE

How else but through a broken heart
May Lord Christ enter in?

OSCAR WILDE (1854–1900), THE BALLAD OF READING GAOL

I saw also that there was an ocean of darkness and death, but an infinite
ocean of light and love, which flowed over the ocean of death.

GEORGE FOX (1624–91)

A Celebration of Spring

The following extracts are from 'A Celebration of Spring' by David Adam, an illustrated volume of personal reflections, poems and prayers (SPCK, 2005). The author of many successful books, David Adam was Vicar of the Holy Island of Lindisfarne until his recent retirement.

'We are Easter people. Alleluia is our song'

AUGUSTINE OF HIPPO

Under the peaty soil life revived

The first time I watched my uncle prune his roses, I looked on in horror. He seemed to be destroying good strong plants. Every snip of the secateurs diminished the plant. There was soon more on the rubbish heap than left in the ground. My uncle explained that this would make for healthier and stronger roses the following year. He also said: 'Pruning them now will protect them from being knocked about by the winter winds. This cutting back is for their own good.'

Years later, I watched the gamekeepers 'burning off' the heather on the moors. The flames attracted me. The heather was perishing in the flames; it hissed as it was burning. These countrymen knew what they were doing; all was planned and under control. The area for burning off was chosen carefully. The heather there had become old and useless, all twisted and gnarled: it had lost its sweetness and no longer sustained the moorland life. So it perished in the flames. The gamekeepers made sure the peaty soil did not burn. For a year or so after the fire, the earth was blackened and lifeless. Then, the following spring, new shoots began to show. The heather had not been destroyed, only its old body. Under the peaty soil life revived: the heath would

> *The human body is a strange and mysterious thing, vibrant with energy and ever changing. Throughout its earthly existence, the body dies and rises again many times and yet the person to whom that body belongs continues. Every single cell carries the entire instructions for a hundred thousand genes. Every minute about a million cells die in our body and are replaced by another million. In the time you take to read this page, your body will have gone through many deaths and resurrections and yet you survive. You are a living miracle. New life is forever blossoming within you. I have no difficulty in believing, if God could design us this way, He could give us the power to rise again and again and give us eternal life.*

return fresh, green and full of sustenance. It had not perished but rose like a phoenix from the flames and blackened earth. Here for me was an image of the resurrection. The old body had been destroyed, yet it did not perish—it rose again to newness of life.

> **It had not perished but rose like a phoenix from the flames and blackened earth. Here for me was an image of the resurrection**

The sun dances

There is a lovely tradition from the Hebrides that the sun dances on Easter morning. Behind this is the belief that the whole of creation is changed by the resurrection of Jesus Christ. Not only the human race but every tree, plant, flower, and every creature of the earth, the air, the sea is raised with Christ. We are invited to join the dance of creation and to rejoice in the risen Lord. ■

Snow on Good Friday

What a blasted day!
Over night young shoots frosted
Cut down by the savage icy wind
And now being buried in snow

The flowers I watched grow
Tender shoots harming no one
Deprived of life in a moment
Now all broken and flattened

I do not want to take it personally
But I find it all frustrating, annoying
A waste of my time and attention
Destruction that does not make sense

Yet on Good Friday, it happened to you
Life broken, poured out, ended
Buried in the ground, like some seed
And you came again, undefeated

Let not the coldness triumph over us
Let not the darkness or bitterness destroy us
Lord, that was cast down, uplift us
Help us rise above this, and to life eternal

DAVID ADAM

Quiet Garden— an invitation simply to 'be'

'What do you do when it rains?' is a question we are often asked when people first hear about Quiet Gardens. They have a picture in their mind's eye of someone sitting in the middle of a lawn, under an umbrella, praying, so they are relieved to discover that the words 'Quiet Garden' are not to be taken too literally. Most Quiet Gardens offer space indoors as well.

'Come with me by yourselves to a quiet place,' Jesus said to his disciples after a particularly busy period (Mark 6:31). Most of us, although we are aware of our need for spiritual refreshment, are not good at taking time out in our own homes and gardens; there are always tasks to be undertaken indoors and outdoors and we feel guilty if we simply sit and do nothing. Having a place nearby to go for a couple of hours during a morning or an afternoon, or for a day, without having to plan it months ahead, can be a godsend. It can also be a gentle introduction to a more formal retreat, as people recognize their need for quiet but are uncertain how to use the time.

What happens in a Quiet Garden? It is a local

Jackie Lock is Administrative Director of The Quiet Garden Trust.

ministry that is offered in response to local needs, so there is a great deal of flexibility. Mostly, the gardens are open occasionally, on specific days. This varies from two or three times a year to weekly, but probably the most common is monthly. Some continue during the winter months; others make the space available only during the warmer weather. Most offer suggestions on how to use the time. Some begin and end with prayers or a led meditation, allowing visitors to spend the rest of the time as they wish; others offer a more formal programme of teaching on Christian spirituality, where participants are led into stillness by a facilitator. A few are available at any time, by appointment, for visitors to 'be' in their own way. Whatever the pattern, all provide a safe context for those wanting to find a deeper meaning in their lives. These may include people who would find a church environment too daunting initially or who, for whatever reason, have drifted away from organized religion.

It was in response to a growing need for quietness that the first Quiet Garden was established in 1992 in a private home by the Revd

Derelict areas have been turned into oases of stillness and beauty

Philip Roderick, the founder-director of the movement. Relaxing in his own garden one day, he recollected that Jesus regularly withdrew to pray in beautiful places on a hilltop or beside a lake. He realized that this was an integral part of Jesus' ministry of teaching and healing. If Jesus himself needed to do that, Philip reasoned, how much more do we all need time to step aside. This is the calling of every Christian, not just for the select few. So the concept of simple low-cost retreats in people's homes and gardens was born. He felt led to name this venture 'The Quiet Garden' after a line in a poem he wrote as an adolescent: 'a falling flower in a quiet garden'. And gardens do feature prominently in scripture as places where people come face to face with God.

By a series of what he describes as 'providential encounters', Philip was offered the use of part of a delightful house, together with the garden, for two days a week. The house is a stone's throw from the parish church of St Giles, Stoke Poges in Buckinghamshire, where Thomas Gray wrote his *Elegy in a Country Churchyard*. A pattern of teaching interspersed with periods of quiet prayer or guided meditation was quickly established, and soon visitors said, 'What a lovely idea! We could do that.' The word spread, Quiet Gardens began to spring up in Britain and abroad, and to date there are well over 260 worldwide, including venues in Ireland, France, Belgium, Italy, America, Canada, Australia and New Zealand, Africa and India.

Hospitality and prayer are at the heart of the Quiet Garden movement

Initially, all Quiet Gardens were at private homes, but soon people began to realize that the concept could be applied in other contexts. Creating a Quiet Garden has transformed the life of some churches as, thanks to the vision of a few people, derelict areas have been turned into oases of stillness and beauty in noisy urban settings. In the process, they have enabled these churches to connect with the wider community. Of course, not all Quiet Gardens connected with churches are in need of so much work. Some are already quiet places and it is a question of making more creative use of existing

> **People come face to face with God**

facilities and naming the space as a place for quiet prayer.

Schools have also created Quiet Spaces, where it is accepted that children and staff can go for some time

> ... a safe context for those wanting to find a **deeper meaning in their lives**

This helps them to move from the mind to the heart, so that they may be more open and attentive and **listen to God**

apart. Often the children and staff have shared in planning and designing the area, and setting the 'ground rules' for its use. These spaces have become an important tool in the teaching of spirituality across the curriculum.

The first Quiet Garden at a hospital came about as the result of a visit by someone working on a Barnado's project in Uganda, who saw how close to burn-out staff at an AIDS hospital were. They were having to cope with the deaths of their patients and their own peers on a regular basis. She felt that they needed a place of beauty close by, where they could go for a few minutes when they had a break. By chance, on her return, she picked up a Quiet Garden

leaflet at St Thomas' Hospital in London (to this day no one knows how it got there!) and, realizing that this was exactly what was needed, she contacted us. Initially we were enthusiastic about the project, but not sure whether the rather English idea of a garden would be acceptable in Africa. It worked, however, and has been much appreciated by those who use it.

Hospitality and prayer are at the heart of the Quiet Garden movement. In Luke's Gospel we are told that Martha welcomed Jesus into her home, thus enabling her sister Mary to spend time sitting at his feet (Luke 10:38). We all need the opportunity to sit at his feet, and this is essentially a simple ministry. Quiet Gardens come in all shapes and sizes, in urban and suburban settings as well as in the countryside. They do not have to be 'show' gardens, nor do they have to be large. One of the smallest was at a terraced house with a pocket handkerchief-sized garden, close to a school and beneath the flight path for Heathrow Airport. Such was the beauty of that small garden, the peace in that home and the warmth of the hospitality offered, that the constant noise was hardly noticeable after a few minutes. There are always sounds to be heard in a Quiet Garden, although visitors are encouraged to be silent. This helps them to move from the mind to the heart, so that they may be more open and attentive and listen to God from the depths of their being. As Paul put it in his letter to the Ephesians, with the eyes of the heart enlightened, we may then begin to know the riches of his inheritance (Ephesians 1:18).

Over the years, it has become clear that there are certain practical criteria which enable a Quiet Garden to run smoothly. If you feel called to this ministry, please contact The Quiet Garden Trust for an information pack. Each Quiet Garden is unique in the way it responds to local needs, but all affiliates share a common purpose in offering a Christian ministry of hospitality and prayer, which is open to all of any faith or no faith, as well as a personal commitment to contemplative prayer. Hosts appreciate being part of a network and of having the opportunity to meet together occasionally to share experiences and resources and to enrich their own spiritual lives.

To find out if there is a Quiet Garden near where you live, please contact the office at Stoke Poges (details below) for a list of telephone numbers.

The Quiet Garden Prayer

(by the 12th-century Cistercian, Guerric of Igny)

O Lord Jesus,
true gardener,
work in us what you want of us,
for without you we can do nothing.
For you are indeed the true gardener,
at once the maker and tiller
and keeper of your garden,
you who plant with the word,
water with the spirit
and give your increase with your power.

Most, though not all, are listed on the Quiet Garden website (www.quietgarden.co.uk), so if you have access to the Internet, have a look there. ■

The Quiet Garden Trust
Stoke Park Farm, Park Road, Stoke Poges
Bucks SL2 4PG
Email: quiet.garden@ukonline.co.uk
Phone: +44 (0)1753 643050
Fax: +44 (0)1753 643081

Julian of Norwich: a garden enclosed

Helen Julian CSF is an Anglican Franciscan sister, a member of the Community of St Francis and presently serving the community as Minister Provincial. She contributes to 'New Daylight' and has also written 'Living the Gospel' (2001) and 'The Lindisfarne Icon' (2004) for BRF.

The idea of paradise as a garden is a very ancient one, found in many faiths. 'Paradise' is from a Persian word, *pairideaza*: *pairi* means 'around' and *daeza* means 'wall'. So a paradise is an enclosed area, whose walls protect a place of shade and water within.

In the Song of Songs, this idea is applied to the beloved, as the lover sings, 'A garden locked is my sister, my beloved, a garden locked, a fountain sealed' (4:12). And later the beloved replies, 'My beloved has gone down to his garden, to the beds of spices' (6:2). The walled garden, enclosed and safe, is a place for love and for encounter.

In the life of Julian of Norwich, too, there was an enclosed place where she encountered God. I doubt, however, that it always felt like a paradise. In her 30s she made a permanent commitment to a life in enclosure, and spent over 40 years in a small hermitage attached to the church of St Julian, near the river in Norwich. After a dramatic church ceremony in which she entered her cell, she was scattered with dust to symbolize her death to the world, and the door was bolted on the outside. She never left her cell after this, and all communication with the outside world took place through two windows, one to the church through which she could join in the Mass, and one to the outside world where people could come to seek her advice.

What caused a young woman to take such a dramatic step? And what purpose did it serve?

Julian (this is not her own name; but is taken from the church where she lived) was born late in 1342. She was probably educated at the Benedictine convent at Carrow, on the outskirts of Norwich, and, as she became the first woman to write a book in English, she obviously used her education well.

In May 1373, at the age of 30, she became seriously ill, and was thought to be dying. Her mother and her priest were called to be with her. In the course of a few hours on 8 May, Julian had a series of vivid revelations of God's love, shown in the passion of Christ. It seems that it was in response to these revelations that she chose to be enclosed, and in her hermitage she spent the rest of her life reflecting on the revelations and writing down the fruits of her meditation.

There are two versions of her writings—one, a short text, probably written down not long after 1373, and the other, nearly five times as long, written as a result of her realization, some 20 years after the original visions, 'that every revelation was full of deep secrets' (*Rev. 51*). She heard God telling her, of one particular revelation, the 15th, 'It is for you to consider all the details and circumstances shown in the illustration; even if you think they are vague and unimportant.' She went on to do the same for each revelation,

It was in response to these revelations that she chose to be enclosed

and in the long text writes that they 'have been renewed by the subsequent enlightenment and touch of the same Spirit (I hope) that showed me them all' (*Rev. 65*).

The 'renewal' included some vivid metaphors, including those drawn from the natural world. The most famous is that of the hazelnut, or, more accurately, 'a little thing, the size of a hazelnut, on the palm of my hand', which God showed her. It represented everything that exists, and she was shown that it survived only by the love of God, which sustains everything in existence.

When she describes the blood flowing from the crown of thorns, she says that its abundance was 'like the drops of water that fall from the eaves after a heavy shower… their roundness as they spread out on his forehead was

Many of us will experience involuntary times of confinement

The 'renewal' included some vivid metaphors

the scales of herring' (Rev. 7). Her enclosure did not close her eyes to the ordinary things of the world.

The 15th revelation may perhaps have spoken particularly to Julian in her 'enclosed garden'. In it she was given a picture of a lord and a servant. The lord sent the servant off to work for him, as a gardener. Julian describes this work as 'the hardest and most exhausting possible'. He was to be a gardener, 'digging and banking, toiling and sweating, turning and trenching the ground, watering the plants for a while' (Rev. 51).

Is it fanciful to see in these words some reflection of Julian's own hard work in digging over the ground of her revelations? The servant in the parable, by his hard work, made 'sweet streams

to flow, fine abundant fruits to grow' (Rev. 51). In her 'garden', enclosed from the world but open to God, she grew her initial revelations into the marvellous book that we know today as The Revelations of Divine Love. What could have seemed a wasted life produced streams and fruits that have nourished many believers, especially since her 'rediscovery' in the 20th century.

The wisdom that came with her years of enclosure was valued by those living around her. Local people left money in their wills to support her life, and it is from one such will that we know that she was still alive in 1416, aged 74.

What has Julian to teach us today? Most of us will never commit ourselves to a life of enclosure, but many of us will experience involuntary times of confinement. As I write, one of my Franciscan sisters is confined to her room with a badly broken leg. She is frustrated at all she cannot do, but it is clear that as she embraces this experience, by the grace of God it is more than her leg that is being healed.

The 'enclosed garden', whether of illness—our own or another's for whom we care—of old age, of poverty, of fear, may become, if we can 'choose' to be in the garden for a time, a place in which God is encountered and our knowledge of God renewed by the touch of the Spirit. ■

The urban garden

The Revd Dave Bookless is UK Director for A Rocha, the international Christian environmental movement (www.arocha.org). He lives in urban Southall with his wife and four daughters, and enjoys Bollywood, bird-watching and biryanis.

People sometimes describe the biblical story as a journey from a garden to a city, from Eden to the new Jerusalem. In reality, the new creation envisaged in Revelation and elsewhere is a garden-city, a place where human creativity and God's creation blend harmoniously. This heavenly city is actually very earthy: it has a river and fruit-bearing trees, and is populated by lions, lambs and snakes as much as by people. God did not create us to exist in sterile urban spaces, but to be rooted in the soil from which we were fashioned. Cities are fine—as long as they contain green corridors, pocket parks, back gardens and touches of

wilderness. Without these, the Babel voices of human confusion drown out the birdsong that feeds our souls. This is not mere pseudo-poetic nonsense: major medical research charities have demonstrated a close link between lack of access to green space and increased incidence of mental health problems.

Spending the 1990s as an Anglican minister in Southall, I became increasingly aware of the damaging effect of a poor environment on the area as a whole—on physical and mental health, on people's lack of optimism, and on their spiritual lives. Around us were graffiti-covered walls, alleyways with piles of fridges and mattresses, and tiny gardens covered in concrete and paving slabs. Yet, as I read the Bible and listened to God's Spirit, I saw a very different vision, of people in an environment where everything around them spoke of God's character and purposes: the birds of the air, the flowers of the field, the rhythms of the seasons. I found myself withering internally if I spent too many days in front of a computer or trailing round a shopping centre—but instantly refreshed by things as small as a walk beside the canal, or a robin on the bird table.

Many of us look at the big issues facing the planet and feel pretty hopeless

It was late 1997 when I 'discovered' a large area of derelict open land on the edge of Southall, an area that I eventually found was 90 acres of greenbelt land belonging to the London Borough of Hillingdon, practically untouched for 30 years—sandwiched between a canal, a dual carriageway and a main railway line. The Minet site turned out to be full of wildlife: the impossible blue of nesting kingfishers, the delicate pink of hawthorn blossom, the unending greens of oak and ash, the subtle oranges and browns of comma and gatekeeper butterflies. The site was also full of rubbish: burned-out cars, deep muddy ruts from motorbike scrambling, whole fields fly-tipped waist-deep with lorry tyres and plastics, and a thrice-weekly fresh anointing of litter from a massive car boot sale. This land became my refuge, a place to disappear to with a pair of binoculars and a Bible, a place where I could shut out the constant roar of traffic, trains and aircraft and become sensitized to the birdsong and the voice of God.

As I listened to God, I sensed something uncomfortable: God was asking me, 'How do you think I feel about this place?' I was reminded of Psalm 24:1, 'The earth is the Lord's and all that is in it', as I looked around at the beauty and the brokenness of creation. Along with my wife Anne, I was already involved with A Rocha,[1] the international Christian environmental charity, and we began to dream dreams. What about an urban conservation project in the name of Christ? What impact would the transformation of a site such as this have on our local community? Would others, like me, experience its healing peace, its smattering of the Creator's fingerprints?

Hesitantly, we began to share our vision with others. Letters to local authorities went unanswered, phone calls passed from one department to another and back again, e-mails bounced off the indifference of officialdom, but, to our amazement, our Christian friends encouraged us to persist. After a while, a few of the seeds we'd scattered began to sprout

into vulnerable growth. Two people in one week suggested that I speak to the local MP for the Minet site, John McDonnell, and I found a kindred spirit—not a Christian, but a man burning with the desire to make his local area better for all its citizens, and a man who saw the value of green space not in cash returns for development, but as a green lung for a choking community. At the same time, a note to A Rocha supporters resulted in Colin Conroy, who had wanted to work in the sun-kissed coastal paradise of A Rocha Portugal, coming instead to live with us in Southall, supporting himself with part-time work while conducting a base-line ecological survey of the Minet site.

Eventually things began to move forward. For so long, our sowing of ideas had fallen on barren soil, but when the seedlings emerged we found ourselves in a rampant tropical garden: we couldn't keep up with what happened next. Within just over four years from Colin's arrival in 1999, we became part of a process that led, by June 2003, to the Minet site being completely transformed, re-landscaped and opened as a country park and conservation area. It was an exhausting, bewildering and exhilarating ride, as if God had swept us on to a great rollercoaster of his mighty purposes. Of course, it didn't always feel like that—not when sitting in three-hour meetings with Hillingdon

...a garden-city, a place where human creativity and God's creation **blend harmoniously**

Council, dominated by party political ping-pong, or when yet another car was set alight in the hedgerow full of ancient oaks. Yet, things kept moving, and mainly forward.

- We registered A Rocha UK as a national charity and named our fledgling project 'Living Waterways', speaking of the canal and the stream, but also of the movement and new life that flow from Christ.
- We were commissioned by the council to undertake a community survey, which showed overwhelming support for open green space.
- We were then asked to do a formal Ecological Audit of the site, and kept discovering new things—over 20 butterfly species, significant numbers of declining birds such as bullfinch and skylark, even nationally scarce water beetles.
- We overcame major opposition when a decision over planning permission for the park was postponed amid the stink of vested interest. In turn, we saw the power of prayer as churches all over west London joined in, and the plans went through unopposed six weeks later.
- I swallowed hard, talked to my bishop, and at the start of 2001 leapt out of parish ministry to head up the project full-time, a decision fully supported by Anne and our growing young family.
- We became a team, growing rapidly to more than a dozen staff in 2005, some self-supported, some living in community, all Christians called to care for God's creation in Southall and around the UK.
- We became the council's partners and advisers as the park was transformed in 2002–03, drew up a management plan for the whole area, and are now contracted, as a Christian charity, to manage the conservation areas, co-ordinate a volunteer warden scheme, and provide environmental education and community activities within the park.

The story of the Minet site and its restoration seems to strike a chord with many people. There is even a professionally-made half-hour video now available![2] We all know soulless urban spaces, and once-green corners that have become society's cesspits. We all know, at some deep level, that God has called us to be gardeners in his creation, to 'till and keep', as Genesis 2:15 puts it—words better translated as 'serve and preserve'. We may also sense, deep within us, a need to put down deeper roots in the place where God has planted us. When we start to dig a garden, to clean an alleyway, to pray around a park, to observe the dates when flowers emerge or birds migrate, we begin to connect with our local environment—the ecosystem in which we are interdependent with other life forms and totally co-dependent on God. In doing this, we are touching something very deep in what it means to be human, to be creaturely and, crucially in a world screaming towards self-destruction, to be good stewards.

Many of us look at the big issues facing the planet and feel pretty hopeless. What difference can we make to the mountains of landfill, the destruction of rain forests, the poisoning of the seas, and the devastation of global warming? Yet, if God could use ordinary unqualified Christians as the catalysts to transform the Minet site, there is hope! Today, as I write, two e-mails have landed in my inbox. One is a statement by the Evangelical Alliance of Papua New Guinea, a place with many wonderful yet threatened species—a commitment by the leading churches to put care for God's earth at the forefront of their mission and practice. The other is from a church conference at which I spoke recently in southern England: 'Dear A Rocha, we have all come home inspired by what was said, and have started a creation care programme within our own congregation.' Today, around the world, A Rocha is finding itself at the cutting edge of a new thing that God is doing in calling people back to the very first commands he gives us—to be good stewards of God's world and our fellow creatures.

When I see the news about melting ice-caps and burning forests, I think of the rubbish-strewn Minet site, and of a bee orchid that emerged in unexpected beauty from a bare bank of soil, a sign of hope. It's a sign too of God's promise that is reiterated in every rainbow—God's promise to Noah, his descendants, and every living creature upon the earth—a promise that God has not given up on his earth, that one day all things in heaven and on earth will find their true place in Jesus Christ. ■

God's promise is reiterated in
every rainbow

NOTES
1   A Rocha is working in 15 countries across five continents to demonstrate God's love for all creation. In the UK it has a membership scheme and, as well as the Southall project, is seeking to stimulate further practical Christian initiatives, as well as to resource churches. For details, e-mail uk@arocha.org or write to A Rocha UK, 13 Avenue Road, Southall, UB1 3BL
2   *A New Creation: Living Waterways in the Urban Desert*: £10 (including p&p) from A Rocha UK.

The Garden

Tony Horsfall is a freelance trainer, retreat leader and author of 'Song of the Shepherd' (2004) and 'A Fruitful Life' (2006) for BRF.

These are conversational prayers, written as a dialogue with God. The idea is to take a scripture and meditate upon it, using the thoughts that come as a springboard for prayer. My hope is that you can make these prayers your own and enter into a dialogue with God for yourself.

Sunday

Now the Lord God had planted a garden in the east, in Eden; and there he put the man he had formed (Genesis 2:8).

So this is where it all began, Lord—in a beautiful garden. Paradise. Trees and fruit; birds and animals. And a river

running through the middle—refreshing, life-giving.

It's a place of rest and communion too—meeting with you in the cool of the day. Sharing, talking, enjoying each other.

Thank you for the glimpses that I still see of you in creation, Lord. Help me to remember that everything you do is good, and that the plans you have for me are for the very best. Forgive me when I lose touch with you in the busyness of life. Bring me back to the place of rest, where my soul is centred on you. Amen.

Monday

So the Lord God banished him from the Garden of Eden... (Genesis 3:23).

What a tragedy, Lord. Paradise gained, and then lost! To have known such beauty, enjoyed such peace, and then to lose it. And yet I do the same, as you well know, Lord. I take your precious gifts for granted. I spoil the good things you have given me. I choose to follow lesser gods.

Yet, echoes of Eden still ring in my heart. I long for what was lost to be restored. Lord, open the way for me to find your healing presence once again. Amen.

Tuesday

Then Jesus went with his disciples to a place called Gethsemane (Matthew 26:36).

Another garden now, Lord, but this time dark and lonely. A place of torment and betrayal. And in the shadows there you are, praying with tears, sweat and drops of blood. Choosing to do the Father's will, no matter what the cost.

How can we thank you, Son of God, for what you did for us? Such courage, such sacrificial love. You were willing to bear the pain and enter hell itself, that we might live again.

Strengthen me in my decisions, Lord. Help me to choose to do what's right, to place the Father's will above my own, to follow gladly in your steps. Make me worthy of such costly love. Amen.

Wednesday

At the place where Jesus was crucified, there was a garden, and in the garden a new tomb, in which no one had ever been laid (John 19:41).

It's sunrise, Lord, and as the darkness disappears Mary comes quietly to visit the garden tomb, supposing you are dead. She does not yet know that the stone has gone, the grip of death defeated by your resurrection life. And when you speak, she thinks you are the gardener, so unprepared is she for such momentous truth.

Lord, you catch us all unawares. Sin removed? Death defeated? Yes, and more besides! Restored again to fellowship with God, a new and living way opened up for us. Thank you, Jesus. Yours is the victory, ours is the freedom. Amen.

Thursday

The kingdom of God… is like a mustard seed, which a man took and planted in his garden. It grew and became a tree' (Luke 13:19).

Thank you, Lord, that the gospel really is good news, and when people respond with faith, a seed is planted within them, full of your resurrection life. And it grows and bears fruit, transforming them.

And it's happening now, Lord, all over the world. Your kingdom is coming. Your will is being done. The gospel is spreading as you said it would.

Let me be a part of it, Lord, sowing seed wherever I go. Help me to water it with my prayers and nourish it with my love. And then, Lord, will you give the increase? Amen.

❖

Friday

You are a garden locked up, my sister, my bride (Song of Songs 4:12).

It's easy to picture my life as a garden, Lord. It is a special place, kept for you and no one else, a place of intimacy, where lovers share the secrets of their hearts. You deserve nothing less than this, O lover of my soul.

Would you help me to keep my heart pure, Lord? To tend it carefully, removing the weeds, keeping it just for your delight?

Will you cause your life to blossom within me? Will you produce in me that lovely fruit of the Spirit? A little glimpse of Eden fleshed out in me.

May the fragrance of my life be pleasing to you, Lord, and attractive to others, so that, enjoying the garden, they may give praise to the one who is the Gardener. Amen.

Saturday

You will be like a well-watered garden, like a spring whose waters never fail (Isaiah 58:11).

Lord, I don't have the energy or the capacity to live for you unaided. I need your help, otherwise I am dry and barren.

Thank you for the promise of your Spirit, the assurance that you will keep on pouring your living water into my soul. Only then will the garden of my life be fruitful.

I depend on you, Lord, every moment of the day. As I come towards the end of this week, would you refresh me again from the river of your grace? And having received from you, enable me to release your life to others whose souls are likewise parched. Amen.

Musings of a middle-aged mystic

Veronica Zundel is a journalist, author and contributor to BRF's 'New Daylight' Bible reading notes. She lives in north London.

In an old joke, a passer-by compliments an old man on his beautiful garden. 'Isn't it wonderful,' he gushes, 'what God and you have achieved together?' 'Ah,' replies the gardener, 'but you should have seen it when God had it to himself.'

Being a garden owner whose little patch is currently left to God alone, I know what the old gardener meant. I must say, God seems to like weeds a lot! I have great admiration for those who are devoted to their gardens. I love to sit in a peaceful garden, especially a convent or retreat centre garden, breathing in the scents and listening to the birds. I'm grateful to those who put their backs, and their patience, into creating these harmonious spaces for others to enjoy.

My mother, though not a Christian, often quotes the lines, 'You are nearer God's heart in a garden than anywhere else on earth.' Why does a garden speak to us so strongly of God, when it's essentially a human creation?

Perhaps the old joke is wiser than it appears. God provides the raw material—the millions of plant species and their seeds, the soil, the sun, the rain—but leaves their cultivation to us. The creation story

... a living symbol of the **partnership** between ourselves and God

Gardens, unlike fields, don't exist simply to feed our bodies

decorative luxury? It's true that, in the past, only the rich had gardens purely for pleasure. For the poor, a garden was a way of growing a little extra food, or most of the food they got. During World War II, those days were revived as ordinary people were exhorted to 'dig for victory' and supplement their meagre rations with homegrown fruit and veg.

Yet still, even in the poorest rural hovels, women (for it was mostly they who gardened, the men being out in the fields) would grow a border of hollyhocks, sweet williams, lupins, forget-me-nots and other old-fashioned perennials, simply for their beauty. Maybe that's the whole point of a garden—that it isn't purely functional. Gardens, unlike fields, don't exist simply to feed our bodies, but to feed the God-given urge to create and appreciate beauty.

in Genesis 1 tells us that human beings' first mandate from God is to care for the earth, to nurture its latent potential, to make it into something that only human beings can.

Whatever your view of the historicity of Genesis, the story's message is profound and challenging: it speaks of a God who is not willing for creation to 'come into its own' without the cooperation and work of humans, the pinnacle of creation.

Is that why we find a garden, whether created by ourselves or others, so satisfying? A garden is, as it were, a living symbol of the partnership between ourselves and God, which is our calling from the moment we became human to the end of time.

But what 'use' is a garden, unless it incorporates a vegetable patch and an orchard? Isn't it just a piece of

If God (as Jesus says in John 15) is the gardener who tends and prunes our lives, the purpose of that gardening may be not just to grow fruit that can feed the world. Is it possible that the gardener God, while rejoicing in the fruit we bear for the harvest of the kingdom, also enjoys just contemplating us with love as we grow (so slowly!) into the beauty of Christ? Does God still enjoy just walking with us in the garden at dusk on a summer evening, when the work is done, and all the perfumes breathe into the cooling air? ■

We want to hear from you...

Thank you to all our readers who have contacted us over the past months. It has been so encouraging to hear your thoughts about *Quiet Spaces* and to see the fruits of your creativity. If you have access to the Internet, do please visit the *Quiet Spaces* website: www.quietspaces.org.uk.

In the next issue, we consider 'The Wilderness'—a place of challenge and adventure, but also a place where we may feel alone, abandoned by God. We will be exploring both the light and the darkness in this theme, discovering how God is with us, even on the hardest of roads.

Contact us at:

Quiet Spaces,
BRF, First Floor,
Elsfield Hall,
15–17 Elsfield Way,
Oxford OX2 8FG

enquiries@brf.org.uk

QUIET SPACES SUBSCRIPTIONS

Quiet Spaces is published three times a year, in March, July and November. To take out a subscription, please complete this form, indicating the month in which you would like your subscription to begin.

☐ I would like to give a gift subscription (please complete both name and address sections below)

☐ I would like to take out a subscription myself (complete name and address details only once)

This completed coupon should be sent with appropriate payment to BRF. Alternatively, please write to us quoting your name, address, the subscription you would like for either yourself or a friend (with their name and address), the start date and credit card number, expiry date and signature if paying by credit card.

Gift subscription name _____

Gift subscription address _____

_____

_____ Postcode _____

Please send beginning with the next November / March / July issue: *(delete as applicable)*

(please tick box)	UK	SURFACE	AIR MAIL
Quiet Spaces	☐ £16.95	☐ £18.45	☐ £20.85

Please complete the payment details below and send your coupon, with appropriate payment to: BRF, First Floor, Elsfield Hall, 15–17 Elsfield Way, Oxford OX2 8FG.

Name _____

Address _____

_____

Postcode _____ Telephone Number _____

Email _____

☐ Please do not email me any information about BRF publications

Method of payment: ☐ Cheque ☐ Mastercard ☐ Visa ☐ Postal Order ☐ Switch

Card no. ☐☐☐☐ ☐☐☐☐ ☐☐☐☐ ☐☐☐☐ ☐☐☐☐ ☐☐☐

Expires ☐☐ ☐☐ Issue no. of Switch card ☐☐☐

Signature _____ Date ___ / ___ / ___

All orders must be accompanied by the appropriate payment.
Please make cheques payable to BRF

☐ Please do not send me further information about BRF publications

PROMO REF: QSGARDEN
BRF is a Registered Charity